THE FIRST LINE
OF DEFENSE

THE FIRST LINE OF DEFENSE

MY LIFE AS AN EMT

TATE YOHE

CHAIRAPY

Copyright © 2020 by Tate Yohe. All rights reserved.

Published by

CHAIRAPY
Enola, PA

Contact Tate Yohe:
www.TateTheBarber.com
TMYohe1@Gmail.com
Instagram: Tate.the.barber

ISBN 978-0-578-82266-2

Designed and printed in the United States of America

This book is dedicated . . .

. . . to my family, my friends, and the amazing men and women I have had the pleasure of working with over thirteen years of prehospital work.

. . . to my always supportive and encouraging wife. I could not have accomplished this without your support.

CONTENTS

	Foreword	1
1	The Beginning	3
2	The Dream Comes True	11
3	The First Line of Defense	17
4	No Longer Green	23
5	Five Stages of Grief	31
6	Feasting With Friends	41
7	SWAT and Funnel Cake	47
8	Grabbing a Handful	53
9	Pranking Gone Right?	59
10	Ride the Lightning	65
11	Back from Death	73
12	Guardian Angel	79
13	Domestic	83
14	Christmas Steak	89
15	The End	93
	Epilog	97
	About Tate Yohe	99

FOREWORD

What's it like to see a dead body?

Whenever I meet someone for the first time, and they find out what I do, this is usually their first question. To the layperson, seeing a dead body weighs heavily on the psyche. For me, it's just commonplace reality, and there is a great deal more to my job than occasionally transporting the deceased. To quote the greatest EMS movie of all time, 1999's *Bringing Out the Dead*, staring Nicholas Cage.

> *I realized that my training was useful in less than ten percent of the calls, and saving lives was rarer than that. After a while, I grew to understand that my role was less about saving lives and more about bearing witness. I was a grief mop. It was enough that I simply showed up.*

The longer I did the job, the more I realized just exactly how true that statement was.

Allow me to introduce myself:

My name is Tate, and I am an emergency medical technician. While some of you may be familiar with what I do, let me fill the rest of you in on my swanky jargon. An emergency medical technician, or EMT for short, is a type of first responder. If someone is going into cardiac arrest, or is having problems breathing, and you dial 911, they get in contact with us, and we come to your rescue.

I have learned many things during my thirteen-year career, some more important than others, but in this book I want to share more than just the knowledge I've acquired. I want to share the stories that built a man, the experiences that shaped a life, and the events that influenced the lives of many others I've had the pleasure of interacting with. We all start out wide-eyed and green behind the ears. There's nothing wrong with a childlike sense of wonder when embarking on a new journey, but knowing that the journey is what shapes us is, I think, one of the most important and overlooked aspects of life. I hope you enjoy my recollections as much as I enjoyed living them.

Chapter One
THE BEGINNING

I often find myself remembering nostalgic childhood dreams involving medicine. It may seem odd at first to assume that someone who was only in the fourth grade would have the ability to understand my longed-for profession, let alone make a decision to pursue it. But nonetheless, this is what happened, even if I was unconscious of it at the time. The obsession took hold from a very early age, and if obsession sounds like too strong a word for a fourth grader, it's the best way I know how to describe it. Even then, sitting in silence during my independent reading time at school, I knew that I was going to go into the medical field. I can still picture those long winter months, sitting in a stuffy classroom with thirty other kids and a teacher who feigned interest in our endeavors to educate ourselves through private reading. During this time students could read anything they wanted as long as they were reading. I have no idea who came up with the system; it seemed like a prime excuse for kids to lounge about digesting the latest comics or adventure books. Maybe they thought this freedom would encourage us to use our imaginations and develop our individual interests. I'm not a child-rearing expert, but what I do know, at least for myself, is that independent reading was a blessing I couldn't comprehend at the time. I was a very cunning young man. With my incredible stealth, I procured some of my stepdads' medical textbooks to read during class. They detailed the skills and knowledge that a paramedic was expected to master and they fascinated me in every way. Every day I pulled out a thick, heavy book and consumed information not really tailored to someone my age. The brains of my peers were filled with dragon quests and flying brooms while I was becoming an eight-year-old expert in scalp lacerations and compound tibial fibula fractures. You could ask me anything—What is the breathing rate of an infant? How can I check someone's pulse?—and I would have an answer. Something about learning body mechanics and pathology intrigued me so powerfully that to this day I cannot fully it. One thing that may shed some light, however, was the environment in which I was raised.

My home was like a cooking pot, perfectly blending all the aspects of the medical field. Marylin, my grandmother, was a lifelong floor nurse at Bradford Regional Medical Center in Bradford, Pennsylvania. I spent many nights sitting with her at the nurse's station asking questions and eating sherbet ice cream. Why sherbet? Because at that time all of the refrigerators in the hospital had small one-portion cups of sherbet for the patients. My mother, Teri, was a respiratory therapist at the same hospital. On days when I didn't have a babysitter I would go to work with her and sit in the break room or a waiting area while she rounded on patients. The other children in the waiting rooms played with toys, but they never captured my attention the way that a spirometer did. Trying to get the little ball inhaled all the way to the top was way more fun than playing with coloring books or building blocks.

One evening, I sat on one of the familiar old waiting-room chairs constructed of some sort of imitation leather that had been worn down by the behinds of many heavy patients. They felt comfortable, like a warm, familiar place where I was safe. One of the most important aspects of medical care is making a patient feel safe, like the way I felt in that waiting-room chair. The hallway was kept half lit to conserve energy (it wasn't the classiest of places). My feet dangled from the chair like the arms of an orangutan. I was bored. There were no instruments to play with and I had memorized the posters hanging from the wall. I knew them so well I could have been the customer service rep.

I strolled to the magazine stand and found an issue that piqued my curiosity. On the cover was a tall, confident-looking man with his arms crossed, standing before an ambulance. His stance was almost heroic, like he was your favorite comic book hero about to take on a villain. He looked so cool. I didn't read anything, I just looked at the picture for a few minutes and returned to my seat where my imagination took me on a wild adventure of rescuing someone in distress.

Jerry, my stepdad, was a paramedic who worked out of the same hospital as my mother and grandmother. He was a kind man with no shortage of friends who enjoyed his company. He and my mom met on the job; it seemed that being in the same line of duty had created something special between them. Jerry didn't have any kids when they met and, as a twenty-one-year-old guy, he had no idea how to interact with children. Bless him! But he did the best he could—he let me play with all his cool paramedic stuff—and I am grateful. It was Jerry who inspired me to become an EMT.

His kit included a bunch of anatomically correct models of hearts, lungs, and brains that you could take apart and put back together. I spent hours each day assembling and disassembling them like I was an architect designing the greatest structure that mankind had ever seen. I learned and studied how each of them functioned before placing them back into the model frame. With his supervision, I was allowed to pull equipment off the medic unit and ask how each piece worked. I guess it was a different sort of time because I doubt a child would be allowed to handle expensive medical equipment today. Among the coolest things I got to mess around with were the defibrillators. A machine that had the ability to bring people back from the brink of death was just astoundingly awesome. My stepdad carried a very old model, the LifePak 10, with detachable paddles. I would pretend to shock patients back to life even though I was never allowed to actually turn the power on. I always found it rather strange how no one seemed to fully trust me with a machine that could generate huge voltages. I thought I was an extremely responsible kid!

Later on, my sister Tiffany became an X-ray technician. It seemed like there was some sort of magic spell attracting every member of my household to the same hospital, even though she eventually moved to Erie to work at Millcreek Community Hospital. Our family's dinner table conversation were like episodes of a medical drama. Discussion flowed from topic to topic and stayed very real and raw because my family predominately talked about work. They discussed the patients that came into the emergency room, the latest equipment they were able to test, and how bad the car crashes were. Luckily for my childhood self, the exact details of injuries were skipped, but things were covered in broad strokes and I started to understand the seriousness of my family's work. One evening, my mom was serving goulash, one of my favorite meals. I think I was around nine at the time. My stepdad had just come home from a late shift and looked exhausted. He plopped down on his favorite chair at the dinner table, still visibly sweaty from his work. "Took care of a real nasty one today, fella had a lot of you-know-what spurting from his head after coming off his motorcycle at speed," Jerry said as my mother served the delicious tomato, meat, and macaroni concoction. He seemed to think that avoiding the word *blood* somehow spared my innocence. Little did he know that his textbooks has already made me a master of all things hemoglobin. They went on to discuss the case at length and I sat there fascinated while I devoured my food. The dream that had taken root in my heart was being confronted by a harsh reality: You can't save someone unless someone's life is in actual danger. It wasn't a game. It was life or death. It's not as though I didn't know this before, but it sank in deeply that night. It was a morbid realization for someone so young, but one that was necessary to pave my path for the future. However, as every young person develops, they start to explore other interests and I was no different. I went through my share of phases, but of course I was *always* perfectly behaved and never got into trouble

The Beginning

(I'll leave out the stories of alcohol and late nights for the sake of those who know me).

Given my exposure to the medical field, you might think that I excelled in subjects such as science and finished at the top of my class, ready to move on to college and a career. Well, I'm sorry to disappoint the type-A personalities, but my life wasn't quite that streamlined.

I honestly had no idea what I wanted to do throughout high school. My childhood fascination had faded a bit and I often found myself drifting, more intrigued by the opposite sex than my academic achievements. One day I met with a guidance counsellor to start thinking about life beyond high school. I was sixteen and it had been a long time since I had given my future career any serious thought. Fortunately (or unfortunately, depending how you look at it), I was told "you have to go to college after school if you want to do anything with your life." As I listened to woeful stories of those who left formal education just to end up in low-income jobs, my mind drifted toward other things. I hadn't eaten yet and I was daydreaming of cooking up something delicious. I had somehow discovered that I had a rather large affinity for cooking. It seemed to come naturally to me, so that day, as I sat in the guidance counsellor's office thinking about how to make the perfect enchilada, I decided that I was going to go to pursue my passion for cooking. I had found my calling at last, but you won't find my name attached to any five-star restaurants. The story doesn't end here.

Chapter Two
THE DREAM COMES TRUE

While I was at Indiana University of Pennsylvania my family moved to Harrisburg. My stepdad had accepted a job at the local community college and, in the fall of 2004, I also moved there in search of work and a place to live. Now Harrisburg may not be the number-one tourist destination in America, but it had personality and charm. I loved sitting by the river and exploring City Island in the evenings. There was always something to do. Though I enjoyed living there, I was never really able to find my niche at work. I hopped from restaurant to restaurant and while I did somewhat enjoy what I was doing, I really felt like something deep inside me was missing. Don't get me wrong, I loved cooking with a passion. But at the end of the day it was just a job, not a life calling or a greater purpose.

But then destiny came knocking at my door. In the spring of 2007, Jerry (my stepdad) suggested that I take the emergency medical technician class at the community college where he worked. Though I wasn't a hundred percent certain I wanted to pursue medicine, the offer did stir some of my childhood enthusiasm. Plus, since he was faculty, that meant reduced tuition! The

The First Line of Defense

next thing I knew, I was enrolled in the accelerated summer program and classes were beginning.

It was an extremely intensive course, but I never felt like I was out of my depth, even though they condensed a huge amount of material into six weeks of Monday-to-Friday instruction. I don't want to sound like I'm bragging, but it all seemed very easy. Honestly, I had been prepared for this training since I was a child. Those six weeks flew by and, before I knew it, I was taking my state board exam. Soon afterward I was a licensed emergency medical technician.

With my license in hand, it was time to find a place to begin my career. I was working part-time at Old Navy unpacking boxes and folding clothes when I finished my EMT course. It wasn't a glamourous existence, but it paid the bills. In the meantime, I quietly sent applications to the local ambulance companies. I was excited by my future career prospects, but I didn't want to get my hopes up to high (nor alert my current manager to what I was doing). But before I could even begin to appreciate how much my life was about to change, I already had my first call back from East Pennfield Emergency Medical Services. Would it really be that easy? My heart pounded something fierce when I spoke with Phil Speck, the EMS chief, and he asked me to come in for an interview. I didn't realize it at the time, but my stepdad's name carried a lot of weight in the emergency-services community. He had an incredible reputation as a prehospital provider, and he was now the director of public safety at the same community college where I took the EMT course.

The Dream Comes True

The interview was scheduled for a day I was supposed to be at Old Navy, but I didn't care. I would use my lunch break to change clothes and high-tail it across town to East Pennfield Township to hopefully secure my first EMS job. That day, when I arrived at Old Navy, I stashed my interview clothes in our common bathroom. The place stank something fierce so most of us would just hold it in until we could go to the bathroom someplace else. I had about an hour to jump in there, get dressed, race to my car, do the interview, and get back. The second the clock hit twelve-thirty I made a beeline for the bathroom. I don't think my supervisor had ever seen me move so fast. Less than three minutes later I was suited and booted and ready to take on the world. I jumped into my old Nissan and streaked across town. On the way, an ambulance with its lights on dashed past me. As a normal member of the public, the best way to help in such a situation is to make sure your vehicle isn't blocking the road. But I couldn't help but imagine what it must be like on the other side of that wheel. At twelve-forty-five I arrived at the building where my future would be decided. Would I go back to packing boxes and folding clothes, or was this the beginning of something greater? I mustered up all the courage I could and pushed through the heavy glass doors to find out.

As I walked inside I passed uniformed employees, their radios chirping. They didn't even notice I was there, probably because so many people simply don't have what it takes to do the job. They're book smart and can pass the classes, but when it comes to practical application they are way out of their depth. I felt a nervous tickle in the back of my throat as I waited. I had rushed to get up the stairs and was slightly out of breath, a testament to the fact that I needed more physical training! To add to my misery, small droplets of sweat trickling along my forehead. This was not the look I wanted to bring to such an important interview. But I had no choice. I steadied my gaze and became laser focused because there is one thing I knew for sure: I wanted this job.

I gave Phil a firm handshake before sitting down. He was an intimidating man with a deep voice and a dry sense of humor. He seemed like someone who had spent a lot of time in difficult circumstances and, if I didn't know any better, I would have thought he was ex-military. However, he was also a very kind man and he never made a big fuss about how nervous I was, even though I'm certain he could see it on my face. He asked me some questions and ran some scenarios by me. To my own surprise I was ready for everything he threw at me. It seemed that all the time studying as a child and reinvigorating my passion now as a young man had paid off.

At the end of the interview he asked me how I knew Jerry Ozog, and I replied that he was my stepdad. I can't say for certain, and Phil never confirmed it, but I believe that last bit of information helped push me over the finish line. One day later I received another call from him while I was folding clothes. When I heard his voice I immediately knew that I would be saying goodbye to the boring boxes and hello to a new life. Phil offered me a full-time position as an emergency medical technician with East Pennfield EMS. I had done it! This was the beginning of a career that would forever change my life and the lives of those I'd meet in the back of my ambulance.

I rushed home after work. I couldn't wait to tell my loved ones that I was about to take up the "Family Business." My stepdad congratulated me and left without saying another word. At first I wondered, is he not excited for me? I was following in his footsteps after all. The least he could do was ask me how my interview went. Moments later he emerged from the other side of the house. He said, "There's one thing every great provider needs: his own stethoscope." He handed me his maroon Littman Cardiology 3, the same stethoscope he'd worn for years when he was an active paramedic. This was bigger than getting hired, he was trusting me with a piece of equipment that he himself had used to save many patients. There was something almost magical about it. I felt untouchable as I draped it around my neck like I'd seen him do so many times before.

Chapter Three
THE FIRST LINE OF DEFENSE

When I began my new life, I was more nervous than a sixteen-year-old girl at the prom. Luckily for me, though, I was surrounded by partners that were always ready to help. While we would cruise around the township, I quickly found that one of our regular stops was at the local dialysis clinic. We were there weekly because someone was always suffering from breathing problems or something similar. It became almost ritualistic to hear the radio sound its usual call for our assistance and this time was no different: "Ambulance 1-1 along with Medic 1 class 1 for breathing problems."

I had already started to settle in at this point, but every new call still made me feel a bit uneasy. Somewhere deep down I questioned whether I was ready to do this kind of work. But my fear turned to excitement when we arrived at the location at the same time as our medic, Ron 'Pap' Wentworth. He was the oldest working paramedic in the county, a graduate of the first advanced life-support class that was ever taught in the Greater Three County Area back in the sixties. He came from a time when equipment was large and cumbersome, and you had to call in to medical command to get permission to give oxygen to a patient.

The First Line of Defense

He was a living legend who had literally seen and done everything in the business, and that experience brought a level of comfort to any EMT who was lucky enough to work with him. I was extremely excited that today would be the day I would witness him in action.

"Hey guys," he said. His persona seemed almost too casual, like an old friend meeting up with his pals at a bar. But it somehow didn't take away from his professionalism. You knew that if something would go wrong, he could switch in the blink of an eye and be ready to tackle the problem.

"Hey man, it's good to see you," I answered back, trying to suppress my excitement. My partner had already walked a few steps ahead, but I wanted to pay special attention to how Pap operated, so I decided to stick closer to him.

We made our way to the basement, where the dialysis clinic was located. The elevator doors opened, and we were immediately hit with the familiar smell of bleach and blood. The first time you enter a dialysis clinic it can be quite intense. Once you get over the aroma, you'll find rows of recliners filled with people tethered to machines like farm animals, all getting their blood cleaned. It was a place of healing, but I wouldn't have liked it as a child. It resembled something from a horror film.

Together with Pap, we made our way down the long corridor to our patient. The gentleman was a large man, roughly four hundred pounds, and unfortunately with only one leg. But he had a warm smile and kind eyes that greeted us when we approached.

Even though he struggled to breathe he still managed to squeeze out a "Hello." I began my assessment while Pap asked questions about how long he had been short of breath. Speed was of the essence in this line of work, and I was attempting to become faster as well as increase my standard of care during my assessments. Pap fingered through the paperwork hoping to find answers for our patient's sudden shortness of breath. It was a common practice, and sometimes we wouldn't find the causalities in this way, but this time was different. Pap looked assured, as if he knew what the problem was, and he placed the patient on the cardiac monitor to take a closer look at his heart. He didn't know it, but I was watching him to see how he would handle this case, trying to learn all I could. After my assessment, I got the stretcher ready for the patient. We had planned to lift him onto it because we didn't want him to exert any more energy and potentially aggravate his shortness of breath. When the patient realized that we were going to pick him up, he refused to let us move him. He exclaimed, "I am too big for you to move me and I don't want you to hurt yourself. I can transfer and move on to the stretcher without help." *Fine by me,* I thought, but I felt some pity at the man's efforts to preserve his pride.

With only one leg and a four hundred-pound body, he stood up and sat down on our litter. He sat there trying to catch his breath for a few minutes, and then he fell over backwards. A very short moment went by, but it seemed like a lifetime. What had just happened? Pap looked at the monitor. The patient had flat-lined. He was pulseless; dead. I couldn't believe it. Just a moment ago this man had sat in front of us smiling, and now his life hung in the balance.

"START COMPRESSIONS," Pap yelled. I ripped the man's shirt down the middle, placed both hands in the center of his chest, and did one compression. Not one and a half, not two, just one solitary compression. And with that one compression, the once-dead patient sat straight up and looked at me like I had three heads and wings coming out of my back. I don't think either of us had ever been so confused. When he looked down at his shirt and saw that I had torn it in two he became angry. It turns out he wasn't too thrilled with the destruction of his brand-new shirt.

In an attempt to capture the moment in words I said, "Sir, do you realize your heart just stopped?"

"What?" he exclaimed, bewildered.

"Your heart stopped and we ripped your shirt to start compressions and attach defibrillation Pads."

I looked at Pap. His eyes were big and round, like golf balls. If we hadn't been in such a tense situation I might have laughed. Trying to make some sense of what had happened, he said, "I guess we should treat this like a post-cardiac event and transport to the closest hospital." The patient reluctantly agreed. Thankfully, the hospital was right next door. We escorted him to the emergency medical wing and dropped him off. As we made our way past the nurses station to get fresh sheets, the doctor came out to greet us. "I thought you said this was a cardiac arrest when you called . . . what happened?"

Pap just laughed with half a grin. "He got better."

Making our way to the ambulance, Pap confessed, "That was the strangest thing I've seen in quite some time."

"Tell me about it. Never seen something like that in my life," I answered, knowing full-well that, at this point, I hadn't really seen much at all. We wandered the rest of the way in silence. We later discovered that the patient's issue was serious enough to warrant a pacemaker. I was glad that we had been right there to spot the issue, because it may have gone unnoticed otherwise.

Even now I think back to my first case with Pap. I had started out so excited and was flung right into the chaos. It was a difficult learning experience, but definitely something that helped me grow as an EMT. And the best part was that even years later I would run into our patient and his family and they always thank me unconditionally. That's a strange feeling, to give someone a second chance at life. I didn't actually do anything special, I didn't use magic or cast a spell. I just did my job and I never expected a thank you. But when I see him now, years after his heart stopped, still enjoying life, I know that I made the right career choice.

Chapter Four
NO LONGER GREEN

Do you know that feeling deep inside your stomach when you're about to do something you don't feel one hundred-percent ready for? I have learned to embrace that feeling because you can't function optimally as an EMT otherwise. Personal growth isn't easy. In fact, many situations force us to grow whether we want to or not! And this time was certainly one of those times. The scene was set for the perfect storm. It was a Friday night with a full moon. If something was going to happen, tonight was the night.

I was still fairly green on the ambulance, but I'd been doing it just long enough to be given more responsibility. Specifically, this meant I could work as a single provider now, an exciting and challenging prospect because it meant I'd be trusted to make more important decisions. In fact, I'd be the only one in the back of the ambulance when we transported a patient. Someone's life would be left to me and *only* me. And the very first time this happened it shook me right down to the core.

On this particular night I was working with Steve Groff, someone who I had great admiration for. He was an average-looking man, not particularly large or small, and one of his few defining characteristics were the silver streaks that garnished the top of his head. However, Groff always walked with a sense of purpose and confidence. You knew that behind his mundane veneer was something more, something deeper. He had been doing this job just long enough to have seen more that the average provider.

Groff was what we call a lifer, which means that he had been an emergency medical technician for the last fifteen years. Most people spend five to seven years as an EMT before going on to be a paramedic or to nursing school. It was a natural progression that most people pursued. However, Groff was different. He was content being a lifelong EMT and because of his level of dedication, he was damn good at it. A provider of his caliber was a calming presence. I knew that if I ever got in over my head he would be right there with a lifeline.

We started our shift at twenty-two hundred hours (ten p.m.). Forty-five minutes into it that familiar sound echoed through the station. I had just managed to get my head into the right space as late-night shifts can often be difficult. Some part of me was still dreaming of what it would be like to get into bed. But the bellowing sound shook me from my daydream and snapped me back into reality.

We had a train horn hooked up to the house siren and I can tell you this thing was no joke. When a call would drop the siren would sound and the train horn would wake the dead. If your alarm clock gives you PTSD, then you have never heard anything like our siren! You can always tell if a call was serious or BS by the nervous excitement in the dispatcher's voice. What goes unsaid can often communicate more than all the words in the world. When this call came in, and the house siren made me jump out of my chair, the dispatcher's voice crackled with exactly the type of shrill excitement that made me know this was a big one. "East Pennfield Township, 83 South, bridge mile marker forty-three, vehicle accident with entrapment and fire, Ambulance Company 1, Medic 1, due . . . 23:45."

This was it. Everything EMT class had prepared me for was coming to a head. My hands were sweaty, and my stomach was in knots. Was I ready for this? Was I ready to see someone on their worst day and hold their life in my hands? Were my skills good enough to get me through it? "Ambulance 1-1 responding," Groff radioed into county. His voice and demeanor never changed, he was as calm and focused as he was ever going to be.

We tore off into the night with the red-and-white lights dancing off the sides of houses as we sped down the road. It all seemed so fast, everything was a blur. My job as passenger was to operate the horns and sirens. It was almost midnight, and at the first intersection I finally had a reason to open them up. I didn't care that people might be sleeping. I flipped the toggle switch and the siren waled. I just vaguely remember passing some cars and thinking about the fact that the people we were about to see were just like those in the vehicles we were passing. No one expects the worst to happen until it does.

The First Line of Defense

I clenched my fist and swallowed my thoughts. I had to be ready for what I was about to face. County advised us we had a vehicle verses a tractor trailer. Occupants of the vehicle were entrapped, and both vehicles were on fire. As we approached the on-ramp to the bridge, I could see it. Smoke had filled the area and the lights from other ambulances refracted through it. It was almost beautiful, taken straight out of a Hollywood blockbuster. But this was not cinema. This was real life and the story is made by the actions of those involved. In this case, that meant me.

The ambulance came to a grinding halt twenty-five feet from the incident. Groff looked at me sternly and gave orders on what to do and how to proceed. His manner and efficiency reminded me of an army general, but our enemy didn't have a face: His name was time.

When he had finished telling me what equipment I needed and what I needed to do, he said, "You got this." An overwhelming feeling came over me. Groff believed in me, and that meant he saw something valuable in me, something I hadn't seen in myself. Those three words gave me the courage to reach deep down and go to work.

I jumped out of the ambulance and grabbed a longboard and the collar bag. I briskly walked toward the wreckage. but it felt like walking in slow motion through a war scene. Smoke filled the area; patients that had once been in the crumpled vehicle laid about the highway with all their various injuries. This is the sort of scenario that calls for nerves of steel. Not everyone is cut out for this. The blood that streaked the pavement and the cries that filled the air that day confirmed this beyond a shadow of a doubt.

I stopped at a patient who wasn't yet immobilized. My training and instinct immediately took over and I was on autopilot. It all happened in a flash, but in reality it took only minutes. I secured the patient to the longboard and was ready for transport. Some part of me believed I had done it, that the mission was already a success.

However, things are rarely as pretty as that. When I turned to get my partner, he was gone. In the chaos and the sea of people, Groff, my rock in the storm, had vanished! I began to panic and question what I was doing. Did I check all the vital signs correctly? Was I forgetting something that I missed during my inspection of the patient? I was gripped by doubt and fear. My breathing became shallow and my head spun. The noise of chattering personnel and sirens echoed through the sky like a stampede of thirsty water buffalo. I didn't know what to do, all I knew was that I wanted Groff to come back.

Seconds turned into minutes and then, out of the blue, he finally returned. "Sorry, I had some things to attend to over there," he said in his usual calm way. I didn't even answer properly, I just nodded in acceptance.

There were too many patients and not enough EMTs. This meant we were going to have to split up in order to transport everyone efficiently. I was going to be alone. Nothing except my own ability would keep this person alive long enough to get to the hospital. The whirlwind of emotions inside me climbed toward the surface. From the outside I was just another EMT, doing his job and getting things done. But on the inside I felt like I was going through a trial by fire, that my measure was being thoroughly tested as if from a place high above.

Before I knew it, fire fighters were loading my patient into an ambulance that wasn't mine, and then we were on our way to the hospital. I didn't know my driver, or what ambulance I was in. Everything was foreign and strange, but I couldn't let that deter me from what was in front of me. I was tasked with the job of keeping this man alive and that is what I was going to do, no matter what. I checked and rechecked my treatments, diligently going over every inch of this person's body, making sure I hadn't missed anything. Being thorough is extremely important when someone's life is on the line. At any moment, the patient's breathing could have become obstructed or he could have gone into shock. I needed to be prepared for any change of circumstances. I couldn't sit on my hands.

The ambulance swung in and out of traffic, siren blaring. Performing precise emergency medical work in the back of a moving vehicle is incredibly difficult. Many of us consider chewing to be too loud a distraction, But an EMT lives in a different reality. The shaking of the ambulance and the bumps in the road could decide whether this patient lives or dies. Luckily, I had an excellent driver and so I was spared the worst.

The facility staff were waiting when I arrived at the hospital. It was like passing the baton after running my leg of the race and feeling grateful that the person running the next leg was faster than me. Doctors and nurses swooped in and removed the patient's clothing like vultures looking for a meal. Seeing them work in that environment made me realize I was part of something larger. I started to deeply appreciate the way in which we all worked together for the common purpose of saving a life. We were a body with different organs serving different functions. I was the hands that had just completed their job. It was a tough situation, but I did everything I could.

As I turned to leave the hospital, still absorbed in my own thoughts, I was surprised to find Groff waiting in the hall. I once again felt deep relief. "Well done on that one. It was seriously tough what you just went through," he said. His looked like a proud father who had just watched his son take his first steps.

"Thanks. It was a bit intense, but I think I handled it well. I hope everything went alright with your patient." I did my best to hide the fact that I was almost giddy. After all, we had just come out of an enormously difficult situation in which lives had been seriously affected. But in terms of a milestone for me as an EMT, this was definitely a high point. And I rode that high for hours, days, even weeks. No one could take that feeling from me. I had entered chaos and emerged victorious. Starting that night, I walked a little taller, spoke with more confidence, and felt at home in the back of my ambulance.

Chapter Five
FIVE STAGES OF GRIEF

There are very few things that will make an EMT move fast. One of them is being dispatched for a cardiac arrest. Those two words will make even the slowest EMTs move with purpose. It had been a quiet day and the heat was at an all-time high. I sat on a bench near my ambulance daydreaming about what I could have for lunch that day. The heat made the day unbearable but, luckily, we had found a place in the shade to hide from its excruciating punishment. We'd already worked some tough cases and hoped to find a few moments of relaxation. However, most summer days for EMTs aren't like they are for other people. And even as the warm breeze came and blew past my face, and children laughed with the excitement of leaving school, the radio began to crackle.

"Ambulance company 1, Medic 2-1 class 1, cardiac arrest." My partner and I sprung from the bench and ran to the ambulance. Cardiac arrest meant someone was literally dead, and it was our job to bring them back. It isn't always possible, but we would do everything we could to make it happen. We rocketed into the vehicle and pressed the gas hard. The next few minutes

The First Line of Defense

were a blur as we darted in and out of traffic to the location. Every second we were on the road was a second too long.

We were first on scene. We jumped out of the ambulance, gear in hand, and rushed towards the front door. We were met by a sobbing teenage girl. My throat tightened as thoughts about the inevitability of what we were about to see rushed into my mind. The girl mumbled something under her breath and directed us towards the residence with her finger. It was difficult to make out her slurred speech so we instinctively followed her inside. On the living room floor was a large man face down on the ground. The TV was still on in the background and I knew that just a little while ago he was in his chair enjoying a day with his daughter. But now he was still, purple from the neck up, and lifeless. It was a cold reality.

We rolled him onto his back and began to assess him for life. There are a few key indicators we use when determining if someone is a viable cardiac-arrest patient or if they were too far gone. One thing we look for is *lividity*. The heart keeps the blood moving. When the heart stops the blood stops moving and settles into the body's lowest extremities or the back if they're prone. Based on our findings, this gentlemen had been gone for some time.

One of the hardest things we have to do in this line of work is nothing. We have a lot of training and we know how to respond to a multitude of situations. But there are times when none of that matters. The hardest calls I've ever been on are the ones where I do nothing.

Our instinct is to act and intervene when someone's in trouble, but it was apparent that this patient was beyond anything we could do to help. It was one of the first times that I was the senior provider on a call, and that comes with a lot of weight and responsibility. The senior provider is given the authority to decide when it's time to stop resuscitative efforts and that is exactly what I had to do. I clenched my hand into a fist and gave my partner 'the look' to stop what she was doing. She knew immediately what I meant. EMTs develop a sixth sense for many things, but I wish this was one I never had to pick up.

I decided that I would have the difficult conversation with the family. However, there was a slight problem. There was no family present besides his daughter, and this may be too much for her to handle without her mother. The poor girl was in the corner of the room crying. She was no older than fourteen and she had to witness something that no one her age should ever have to see.

The patient's wife was at work, and this presented a challenge in itself. I somehow needed to get her home without telling her that her husband had died. This was going to be tricky, but I made the call. "Hello, this is Tate from East Pennfield EMS. I'm here with your husband, we need you to come home as soon as you can."

"What's wrong?!?!"

"There's no need to be alarmed, come home as soon as you can, and we'll be here when you arrive."

"Ok, I'm on my way."

I hung up the phone and exhaled a deep breath of relief and pain. Calling the family is always one of the toughest parts of the job. Some small part of you just wants to cry in sympathy, but the nature of the job is to remain professional and that's exactly what I did. I started to become pretty good at it, too. I was no longer the newest guy around, and it was times like these that helped me mature.

Soon the whole family started to arrive. Uncles, aunts, and cousins flooded the yard like a typical family reunion. It was great to see how much support was here for the family. Despite this response, not a single person wanted to go inside, not that I could blame them. The patient was still on his back in the living room. We had made the decision to leave him there until the wife came home. We felt she needed to see him and be with her husband one last time before we called the funeral home. Making decisions like this was also part of the job. An EMT has to deal with situations that most people never witness and be able to think on his feet to adapt. It isn't enough to just learn facts from a book. Discretion was an important part of success.

After twenty-five minutes I finally saw the wife's car pull into the driveway. In the time it took her to drive home, around thirty friends and family had gathered outside, all in the knowledge of what had happened. And when she got out of her car she immediately knew too. Before I could introduce myself, she began to cry. I didn't have to say anything.

Elizabeth Kübler-Ross, a psychiatrist who specialized in grief studies, classified grief into five stages: denial, anger, bargaining, depression, and acceptance. It usually takes someone a few months to go through all of them, and some even require counselling. I wasn't prepared to see this lady to experience all five stages right before my eyes. First there was denial. From the time the newly widowed wife got out of her car she kept repeating, "No, no, no. He's not dead, he can't be dead." Is this some kind of joke, are you kidding me?" At one point she began to laugh as if her late husband was quite the jokester and this was one of his epic pranks. I began to go into what happened and why we chose to stop our resuscitative efforts, but she cut me short demanding to see her husband. I wanted her to understand the gravity of what she was about to see but she didn't care about anything I had to say at that moment. She only wanted to see her husband.

When I refused to let her see him until she calmed down, she entered stage two: anger. She became violent and began to curse and swear, throwing her fists around in the hope of connecting with anyone or anything. I couldn't take it personally; I had no idea what this woman was going through, but I had to remain professional and caring. It was a miracle that she didn't hurt anybody. I tried to reflect on the situation to understand what she must be going through. It's different when you're the observer and it isn't your family member who has passed away.

Eventually, her anger subsided and her family was able to talk her down to a less aggressive place. After careful thought I agreed to take her inside to see her husband. While I was tending to the wife, my partner was able to clean up the patient so that when she came to see him it wasn't so traumatic. No one wants to see their loved one with tubes coming out of them half naked and dead. He was cleaned up and draped with a sheet to protect his dignity.

As we entered her house together, the third stage of grief came on like clockwork. Turning nervously into the living room she began to bargain aloud, saying, "Take me, please take me, I can't do this without you. You just retired, and we were supposed to travel together. Please don't do this to me, come back." She grabbed the sheet that covered her lifeless husband and ripped it off as if she were a magician and, under the sheet, she would find her husband alive and simply playing a joke. It was in this moment that I felt her deep sense of pain and instant feeling of being alone. This was her new reality and there was nothing she could do to avoid it. She laid down next to her husband and ran her fingers through his hair while she muttered memories of the two of them. It was as if they were together on a beach somewhere and falling in love all over again. She hugged and kissed him, refusing to let him go under any circumstances. At that moment she believed she could wish him back to life. She couldn't.

The bargaining became depression. She was motionless and didn't say a word, her head on his chest as if she was listening to his heartbeat, and they were in a field somewhere with the sun setting and the wind gently blowing over them. It was obvious these two had spent a lifetime together full of love and magical moments and she wasn't ready to let him go. Time passed and the silence was deafening. Even though there were people outside muttering, it seemed as though the atmosphere in the room swallowed every sound and dragged it into an abyss of pain.

To my surprise, after thirty minutes of being with her husband, she jumped up off the floor and pulled the sheet back over him. "Go ahead and take him," she said. And just as quickly as it had all started, we had entered the fifth stage: acceptance. She had made her peace.

Typically, I don't let family stay and watch us package the patient before taking them to the funeral home, but I made an exception for his wife. She had just lost her soulmate, she needed to make sure we would treat him with respect and give him the dignity he deserved. One thing that I have found, when transporting the deceased, is to put a pillow under their head when they're loaded on our stretcher. The family sees this and it gives them comfort knowing that they're leaving their loved ones in the capable hands of someone who cares.

We passed many gloomy faces as we wheeled him out of the house. His daughter was still sobbing in the corner of the yard, unable to fully comprehend what had just happened. The place was surrounded by supportive people, but no matter how much they wanted to help, none of them could give this family what they really wanted: some more time with their loved one.

I have come across many patients during my ten years of prehospital work, and I've experienced thousands of life-changing moments, but there aren't many calls that etch themselves deeply into my memory. This one is different. Something about the sadness that this family experienced affected me deeply. I'll carry this experience with me for the rest of my life.

There's an old saying in EMS: "All that's left is the clean-up and the come-down." We had cleared the call and we were back at the station cleaning and restocking the ambulance when I was overcome with a wave of emotion. I, too, was in the middle of something very personal, and this call hit home. My late brother-in-law Eric was going through chemo treatment for leukemia and his prognosis wasn't good. In an instant I could see my sister being that wife, weeping over the loss of her soulmate. As an EMT I am expected to compartmentalize emotion and separate myself and my home life from work, but I couldn't. That evening I left work early and went straight to my family's house to spend time with them and Eric. The one thing we never get enough of is time, and I wanted to spend what time I had with the people I loved.

Chapter Six
FEASTING WITH FRIENDS

DISCLAIMER: Some shifts are not filled with horror and tragedy. A good portion of our time is filled with fellowship and food. If you want to know all the best places to eat, ask someone who works in an ambulance. I guess it's the nature of the business: We can never sit down long for a meal, so we know where to grab a quick bite. I personally love being free on the road. I don't think I would have made it far if I had to work in a stuffy cubicle.

One evening in November, my partner and I decided to put a stop to bad eating. We had spent weeks having one greasy meal after another. And while they were delicious, and my tongue thanked me continuously, I could see myself slipping into a pattern I didn't enjoy. As if by design, this realization came at the perfect time to make a change: Thanksgiving.

It was rather warm for that time of year and it inspired us to do something extra special. I turned to my partner and said, "We should throw a Thanksgiving meal!"

At first, I was met with a glance that reminded me of my teacher when he saw me reading my heavy medical textbook:

The First Line of Defense

disbelief and slight worry. "I don't know, do you think everyone would even bother showing up?" he finally retorted, once the idea had sunk deeper into his mind. Honestly, I wasn't really sure, but this wasn't going to stop me as I knew there were approximately seven ambulances stationed within a twenty-mile radius, filled with potential attendees. I took the initiative and planned the meal ferociously. Overcome by my holiday spirit, my partner soon joined me. We made phone calls to everyone we could and, to our joy, the idea was taken with enthusiasm by our colleagues. I glanced out the window. The November breeze and rustling leaves would be the perfect backdrop for our very own EMT Thanksgiving feast.

We were meticulous organizers and knew how to delegate. Every ambulance was tasked with a different assignment, and my partner and I gave ourselves the ultimate responsibility of providing the turkey. I know what you're thinking: *Why are they giving themselves the most important task? Do they not trust their colleagues?* The short answer to that is *no,* not when it comes to picking out the best kind of meat (Remember, I did go to culinary school!). We had a special knack for that and considered ourselves connoisseurs, so we reserved that responsibility for ourselves.

It was the beginning of third shift, ten o'clock p.m. I loved my usual Thanksgiving tradition of meeting up with my family and chowing down something fierce. But this time I was at work and I had to create something special myself. We wanted to take advantage of the unseasonably warm climate and decided that there would be little that could beat an outdoor meal. My partner had come up with the idea that the large parking lot next to the hospital would be perfect for what we were planning. I was against the idea. After all, the setting didn't really provide the kind of family atmosphere that I had hoped to achieve. But luckily, we thought of a trick that would give us exactly what we needed.

One by one the ambulances arrived, and in order to create our dynamic Thanksgiving setting we parked in a circle, shielding the dining area like a small fort. When all the vehicles were in place they provided a sense of calm that could be felt by every member of our team. EMTs spend most of their time being called to someone else's need, and it becomes difficult to feel like you can have a moment of peace, but somehow that shield of vehicles managed to do exactly that.

Everyone pulled their stretchers out and placed long boards on them to create a firm surface for our buffet table. Clean sheets from the ambulances served as tablecloths. One crew brought mashed potatoes, another green bean casserole, then one showed up with stuffing, another with bread and butter, and one brought desserts, plates, and silverware.

Finally, it was the moment that everyone had been waiting for. We had managed to secure a fantastic looking turkey that would be more than enough to satisfy the crew of seven ambulances. My partner and I pulled out the turkey for everyone to see and placed it in the middle of the setup. Everything was ready.

The First Line of Defense

We took a moment to appreciate what we had created and began to imagine what it would be like to enjoy the incredible feast before us. Thanksgiving is a time to be thankful for the things we have in life, and in that moment I felt extremely thankful. I had gone from being an unfulfilled chef, to a low-paid clothes-folder, to saving lives and being surrounded by some of the most dedicated people I could ever be lucky enough to meet. I looked up at the evening sky and held back a goofy smile at the thought of my life and the joy I felt because of it.

Fourteen people stood in silence while I said a prayer for the food we were about to enjoy. I don't know if it was a sign from above or just luck, but for the next hour not a single person in the county called 911. It was our very own Thanksgiving miracle, and it gave us a much-needed chance to relax and enjoy our feast without stuffing it in our mouths and running to the next call. We all loved our jobs, but sometimes a person just has to sit down, eat, and laugh. And it was a fantastic experience. In this profession we don't have co-workers, we have family, and the truth of it is we sometimes spend more time with this family than we do our own.

"Hey, isn't this kind of crazy?" I asked my partner as he pushed another spoonful of mashed potato into his mouth.

"What do you mean?" he slurred through a mouthful of food.

"I mean, look at this circle of ambulances. Isn't it like when you were a kid and you would use pillows to make a fort?"

My partner looked at me like he wanted to appreciate the thought but couldn't quite grasp it. I don't blame him. Each of us was different and unique. What had brought us together was a passion for helping people. It was an odd group of personalities, I'm sure, and if you had been standing on the outside of those ambulances, listening to us laugh and joke around, you would have found us weird, but it's moments such as that night, and the constant support of those around me, that shaped me into who I am today.

Chapter Seven
SWAT AND FUNNEL CAKE

Autumn is one of my favorite times of the year. The intensity of the summer heat had just disappeared, replaced by a cool breeze. It's usually a time that I use for personal reflection as things start to slow down in the run-up towards the holiday season. But this time things would be slightly different. It was a fresh October day and I had a new partner working second shift with me. Tony was new to our ambulance, but he had been an EMT for a few years before joining East Penn. He was pretty fun to be around, but I could tell he felt as though he needed to prove himself with us. After all, there's a friendly rivalry within the profession. It helps keep us sharp and as good as we can be.

There was a local festival called pumpkin fest going on in town and we were tasked with standing by at the event. This meant we had to sit and watch people stuff their faces and ask us stupid questions like, "Have you ever seen a dead body?" I think I've been asked that question more than a hundred times throughout my career. It's difficult to blame people for their curiosity, they see the uniform and they get intrigued. We live in slightly different worlds, but that doesn't mean it doesn't get annoying.

Tony and I sat on small plastic chairs overseeing the event. There were orange-colored decorations everywhere, children ran throughout the small park, and people contorted themselves in order to win prizes for their kids and loved ones. I looked over at Tony and saw that he had a stern look in his eyes. I was going to ask if he was okay, but I decided to let him stir in his own thoughts. After all, everyone was running around having fun while we sat there doing nothing.

Thank God for small miracles. Just a few moments later the radio crackled and out came that familiar phrase: "East Pennfield Township, staging on Erford Road with police for a possible psych patient."

I leapt at the opportunity. "THIS IS OURS! Ambulance 1 responding."

"Ambulance 1, we have a male patient who has himself locked in his house refusing to come out for police. They believe he has weapons, switch to ops three for command." I felt like the hero in an action movie on his way to take down an enemy compound. Me and Tony jumped up from our personal plastic hell and rushed towards our ambulance. We hit the street with sirens blaring and as we turned the corner, I was glad to be rid of the festivities. All the personal joy I would have gotten from the event had been sucked out by nosy questioners. We arrived on scene just as the sun was going down. The night sky was painted with a spread of vibrant colors. There are sights that can take you out of the moment, and seeing the illuminated horizon was one

SWAT and Funnel Cake

of them. It felt strange; The juxtaposition of the beautiful backdrop and the violent gunman. Never should two forces such as these be intertwined in such a way.

We hadn't been given much information for this case, all we knew about the patient was that he had a mental break after his wife left, and when police tried to make contact he locked them out and said he had guns. Though I empathized with his emotional distress, the man had placed himself and all those around him in a very dangerous position. No one could take any chances, so this called for more than municipal police. It meant SWAT was coming. While we waited, Tony and I perched ourselves against the ambulance to talk about the job. Tony was full of questions and eager to learn anything that I was willing to teach. "What would you do in a situation where an officer and an assailant were both down and injured and you had to choose which one to treat first?" he asked.

"It is always a matter of who has the worst injuries, not the kind of person the patient is. We have to see all those who require medical attention the same way, even if we don't feel like it." I answered.

Before I could continue, I looked up and realized what had happened during our conversation. We had gotten so wrapped up in what we were talking about that we hadn't realized we were by ourselves. All the emergency vehicles that had previously filled the streets were gone and we were alone with the neighborhood cat, awkwardly sitting in the middle of the street. With SWAT arriving on scene, everyone had cleared back at least three blocks but forgotten to tell us (Got to love the camaraderie). Tony began trying to find out information on the radio as I noticed a rustling from the tree line next to the ambulance. A man stepped out from the vegetation in full military camouflage and a long rifle slung over his shoulder. For the first few seconds my heart skipped a beat as I remembered that the man who had locked himself in the house would likely have shotguns. In less than a second he pointed at the ambulance and made a hand gesture telling us to get out of the hot zone, the area directly in front of the patient's house. This was embarrassing. I had just been enriching a junior with my vast medical knowledge and now I felt like I had just confessed my love for a girl in the middle of my tenth-grade classroom. However, I managed to overcome my personal feelings and we jumped into our rig without any questions. We simply put it in reverse and floored it. We arrived back at the main staging area where we were not spared any laughter. It was like we were the main act during an NFL half-time show. Blood rushed to my face, but I played it off as a simple mistake. Luckily, on this day we were not the main attraction. With the arrival of SWAT an intensity lingered in the air. Something crazy could happen at any moment so we had to be on standby. Minutes turned to hours as we played the waiting game. Eventually, SWAT was ordered to just go in after the patient. I watched in amazement as they donned protective vests and loaded their guns.

Now I really felt like I had arrived in that action film. SWAT stacked up on the front door and with a large *POP*, explosives blew the door off and in they went. Everyone waited, expecting to hear an exchange of bullets. However, unbeknownst to anyone outside, the man who had occupied the house was gone. Did he crawl through an escape tunnel or dress up as a member of SWAT to make his great getaway? No, he had simply slipped out the back door and disappeared into the woods. I have to wonder whether he was a mastermind or just plain lucky, but he had managed to outsmart all of us. All that was left from that excitement and anticipation was a big pile of nothing. A whopping disappointment. Well, at least everyone had forgotten about our little mishap! Sometimes it's the small things that matter.

Later that day, when everyone was cleaning up and packing away the equipment, someone showed up with a box of funnel cakes from pumpkin fest. The entire situation was comedic, like a skit that had been designed to be played on daytime television, the incident had devolved from a high stakes standoff to eating baked goods in the street. I have to say that, of all the evening's excitement, my favorite memory is sitting in the middle of the road with Tony, surrounded by police and SWAT, eating leftover funnel cake.

Chapter Eight
GRABBING A HANDFUL

Most people don't enjoy working on Fridays. To them, it's the last hurdle that needs to be overcome before they can finally enjoy a relaxing weekend of doing whatever they want to do. I'm different. For an EMT, Friday night is a night of adventure, one that holds mysteries and incidents I could never have imagined. And this Friday would be no different. My partner and I had just settled into our comfy chairs after prepping our ambulance for the shift. A task I'm usually not too fond of, but it's all part of the procedure. As soon as we got settled in our chairs the radio rang out with its usual gusto. "Damn it, we just got comfortable!" I exclaimed. I could tell by my partner's exhausted look that he thought the same thing. You can't judge us for being tired. After all, it was late in the evening when normal people would be getting ready for bed.

I got used to being uncomfortable because county always seemed to have a way of knowing the exact moment you wanted to settle down. I often wondered if they planted some sort of tracking devices into the cushions of our chairs. However, before the 007 fantasy in my head could fully mature, I was interrupted by the radio again: "Ambulance 1 class 2 for a fall victim."

Without further hesitation we were off into the night, our red and white lights dancing off the houses as we passed. There was always something magical about rushing to an incident. We hadn't been given much information about what we would face. All we knew was that we were heading to a bar for a female who had fallen. One part of the job is always being prepared for anything. A fall could be something minor and exaggerated, especially if alcohol was involved, or it could be a major incident. We were about to find out.

We were met by the bar owner at the scene. It was a wild Friday night and the crowd flowed out of the main entrance and all over the sidewalk. I had been here before to celebrate some events, and it had always been a fun time, the staff was nice, and the atmosphere was uplifting. As I scanned the area, I recognized some of the regulars mingling with the weekend crowd. The sea of drunk people swelled and moved like an organism trying to envelop us. Most of them seemed completely unaware that there had been an incident and just went on to enjoy their night as usual.

As we wandered through the crowd I accidently bumped a rather large man whose face and neck were covered in gang-related tattoos that looked like they had been carved with a rusty nail and some charcoal. "Excuse me," I murmured as I attempted to keep up with the owner as he walked through the building. I was met by an unrelenting stare that pierced through the back of my skull. Much to my pleasant surprise, though, the sight of my uniform made him smile and lower his gaze. He quickly turned away, seemingly frightened. I think that, under the thick influence of alcohol, he mistook me for law enforcement. Who knew that my uniform could come in so handy?

We escaped the crowd, singing nineties music completely out of tune, and made it to a back door. I felt slightly perplexed as we arrived in a yard behind the bar. I glanced to the right and saw a path that led from the front of the building straight here to the back. The hassle we had just gone through to get here has been completely unnecessary. I had risked my life for nothing!

My confusion didn't have time to fester, however, as my partner and I were greeted by the foul words of a very drunk woman sprawled on the ground, covered head to toe in dirt and tears. I felt really sorry for her. Saying she was a bit of a mess was an understatement; her mascara was smeared with the drunken tears of a broken heart. However, my feelings of empathy were perfectly matched by my partner's smart-ass remark: "How'd ya get down here?" he asked through a half smile as he stooped down to assess the situation.

"I was arguing with my boyfriend up on that deck"—one story off the ground—"and I told him 'If you don't stop cheating on me, I'll jump off this deck!' He said, 'No you won't.' So I jumped!" I would have said her story surprised me, but after having been on this job for a while, and having worked many Friday nights, it all seemed perfectly normal. Overall, she was actually in pretty good shape considering the distance her body had plummeted. Unfortunately, though, her wrist had not been so lucky. It was definitely dislocated and posed at a perfect ninety-degree angle from its normal position. As we completed our assessment and checked for other injuries, a crowd had gathered around us. Someone must have spotted the ambulance out front and rumors of a failed romance ending in tragedy spread around the facility.

We managed to package her up quite well and travelled back towards our vehicle at speed. Some people threw drunken questions at us as we made our way back through the bar. It isn't our job to engage with the public, but I have to admit, I was tempted to make an inappropriate joke at the expense of those in an alcohol-induced haze. Luckily, I had become slightly more mature than that after years as an EMT.

We had agreed to meet with a medic while en route due to the patient's needing for a trauma center. I had drawn the short straw and was tasked with keeping her calm. Though I tried my best to be supportive, it was difficult to make out most of the things she said. I wondered how many cocktails she must have consumed, but I was also glad for her because the alcohol was obviously numbing the pain of her wrist. Her heart, however, seemed to be sincerely wounded.

After about ten minutes of driving we picked up our medic. He met us with a dry "Hello" and jumped into the back of the ambulance. Our patient didn't seem to mind his melancholy expression, though, and seemed glad to be surrounded by medical personnel. Her reaction might have been different if she had known what was about to happen next.

Before we could continue to the trauma center we needed to set the her wrist back to its anatomically correct position in order to restore blood flow. This was vitally important if we wanted to avoid any further damage to her hand. Imagine the patient on her back with me immediately to her left and my partner on her right. While I was comforting her, he had been tasked with repositioning of her wrist. "On the count of three you're going to feel a pop," he said. "One, two, POP!" he twisted her wrist back to its natural position. I have never broken a bone or even had a dislocation, but when I see the agony on a patient's face when we reposition a wrist or shoulder, I thank the heavens that I haven't had to endure that torment. Unknowingly, though, I was about to experience something far more feared by any man.

"SWEET BABY JESUS, PLESE LET GO!" I screamed. In that moment of extreme pain, she reached out with her left hand to grab anything she could get her fingers on. Unfortunately for me, and to the amusement of the medic, the thing she managed to grab was my manhood. The agony rushed to my head as the patient squeezed with all her might. When she released me I dropped to my knees and felt so nauseous that I didn't know which way was up. Luckily, though, I was surrounded by a

The First Line of Defense

supportive team of work colleagues who wouldn't stop laughing. Even the patient, after her wrist was back in place, had a good laugh. Energized by everyone's support, I spent the remainder of the transport relegated to the bench with an ice pack on my crotch.

Lesson learned: Don't stand in grabbing distance while putting a person's wrist back in place.

Chapter Nine
PRANKING GONE RIGHT?

One very important skill set not taught in class is the art of the prank. Pranking and EMTs go hand-in-hand like Narcan and Opium (a little bit of medical humor for you). I was working the 14 station one weekend with Ryan Mathews. We had quickly become great friends because we both shared an evil sense of humor and we were spending the next twenty-four hours working together.

The chaos that was about to ensue was guaranteed.

It was a slow day. There had been no major incidents and we were starting to feel the weekend blues. It was prime time for a bit of fun. I leaned over to Mathews, ill-intent oozing from my mouth. "I think we should mess with Andrew today." The new guy who had started work a few weeks ago was just out of earshot.

Mathews grinned from ear to ear and said, "Let's do it!" And so we snuck off to plan our evil endeavor. Andrew was a good, honest worker and always did his best to stay on everyone's good side. I admired that about him, but no one is immune to an EMT prank, and the new guy is always the target. You can

The First Line of Defense

think of it as a type of initiation ceremony, a rite of passage to become a true member of the team, and we didn't want Andrew to miss out. Mathews and I spent the whole morning crafting the most diabolical prank we had ever thought up. In the fire-house showers, the shower heads were detachable and connected by a long tube. We dumped Jolly Rancher candies into a coffee grinder and filling that plastic tube with powdered candy. Then took a bottle of 10% lidocaine and added it to his shampoo bottle. Our hope was that every time he showered he would get extraordinarily sticky so, he would shower again, and again, and again. Every time he jumped into the shower to wash off the stickiness, he would use his shampoo-and-lidocaine cocktail. It was a foolproof plan.

At about ten a.m. we spotted Andrew heading for the showers. Eager with excitement, Mathews and I snuck towards the entrance to catch a glimpse of our fantastic work of art. Other members of the crew had learned to ignore our antics, so they didn't give much thought to us lurking near the shower entrance. Our anonymity came in handy because as we waited we finally heard what we had been waiting for. "What the hell is happening!?" bellowed from the showers. Mathews and I broke down in silent laughter and retreated to a safe distance, awaiting our victim's arrival. Andrew eventually emerged having probably attempted to clean his body more than ten times, screaming, "I'm sticky, and I can't feel my head!" The laughter turned from silent to booming. The whole neighborhood must have heard us, though the others around the fire station acted with more class, quietly chuckling about Andrew's predicament. The plan worked perfectly; it couldn't not have been any better! But our laughter had given us away and Andrew directed his roaring anger right at us. He may have called us names that aren't appropriate for young readers, so I shall keep those details to myself. But the feeling eventually returned to his head and, after one more shower, this time with a candy-free hose and a different shampoo bottle, he was sparkling clean. It didn't take long for our laughter to infect Andrew, and the whole ordeal was soon a moment of true bonding between us all.

Blowing off steam like this may sound juvenile, but the work of an EMT is difficult, full of hardships, and it sometimes places us in the midst of some of the most stressful and emotionally difficult situations imaginable. Pranking does a lot more than just embarrass someone. It creates unity in laughter and helps to lighten the mood in an environment filled with struggle. And so I have continued my prankster ways throughout my career.

Another classic I was privileged to take part in was the old powder-in-the-vents prank. It was the middle of summer and we hadn't turned a wheel in hours. Anyone in emergency medical services knows that this makes for idle time, and with idle time comes idle trouble. The sun was beating down on us as if in a fit of vengeance. Motivated by our boredom and rising body temperatures, my partner and I decided to fill our time with something worthwhile.

Amanda was a young woman who was new to EMS, and we could tell she was new because she left her car unlocked. A

The First Line of Defense

rookie mistake. While she was out on a transport, my partner and I took a bottle of foot powder and dumped it into her car vents. That evening, when she returned from the transport, she clocked out and left . . . but nothing happened. In fact, nothing happened for months! We figured maybe we messed up, maybe the powder fell out, or maybe she never turned on her air. In any case, we felt as though we hadn't just let ourselves down, but that we had failed the entire pranking community. Spurred on by our failures, my partner and I decided that next time we would never fail again.

Fast forward to the end of November. The weather was finally cold enough to use the heat. My partner and I were sitting in the station watching television. It had been a quiet day and we were on a break. I was just daydreaming about what I saw on the screen when the outside door opened and slammed. I immediately jotted around to see what had motivated someone to close the door with such force. I could hardly believe my eyes. Standing there with fury in her eyes and her feet on the warpath was Amanda, covered from head to toe in white powder. She would have made a fantastic extra for "Winter Wonderland." I knew that I was the one to blame for her predicament and burst out Laughing. "Finally!" Touting ourselves as pranking geniuses, we began to calm a rather agitated Amanda and assured her of the innocent intent behind our joke.

However, we had failed to realize that the powder we used in our amazing prank was foot powder with an anti-fungal additive. An honest mistake any prankster could have made, but

Amanda's eyes were watering, and she began to hyperventilate. Our joy suddenly turned to concern. Had we gone too far? We were trained medical personnel, but we weren't experts in this type of thing. Someone suggested we call poison control. I dialed the number and began explaining what had happened. The lady on the other side of the phone laughed as if she had taken this call before. She assured me that what we had done would have no serious consequences. When all was said and done, Amanda was in the shower fuming at us. Apparently, a good wash was all she really needed.

She didn't speak to us much in the following weeks, and I honestly couldn't blame her. After all, this may have been one of the best—or worst—pranks we had ever pulled. At least some of us had a good laugh.

Chapter Ten
RIDE THE LIGHTNING

It was my normal Friday-night shift and I was working with Ronnie, one of the most dedicated people I have ever met at EMS. Ronnie wasn't just a part-time EMT, has was a *lifelong* part-time EMT. This may not mean much to the average person, but to me it always showed a dedication to other people's welfare that I have yet to see in many others. I still aspire to it myself.

Ronnie spent the nine-to-five hours molding young minds as a high-school teacher. He often told stories about how his students would try to sneak out of class when his back was turned, or would try to skip out of P.E with badly written sick notes. His stories transported me back in time to a place where things seemed simpler and I was busy getting into trouble . . . I mean, writing the perfect book report.

The amazing thing about Ronnie was that he dedicated every weekend to 911, answering calls on the ambulance. I couldn't remember the last time he had actually missed a day at work and as he got on the ambulance that evening, I greeted him as I did every weekend. He seemed jolly and in high spirits, so I asked him what he was so happy about. He beamed at me from across the vehicle. "One of my students asked me what I get up

The First Line of Defense

to on the weekends, and I got to tell them about my work here on the ambulance."

I could tell that this had been a first for him and he must have felt like a superhero revealing his secret identity for the first time. The thrill of sharing the exciting experiences of his double life made him ecstatic. "I'm glad they take an interest in stuff like that," I said. "When I was their age, I was busy thinking about how to score some booze without my parents finding out."

Before he could critique my childhood antics, we were interrupted by the radio. We were on our way to West Fairview, commonly referred to as *The Zoo*, for a sick person. It may be an odd name, but it was one that perfectly described the place. Getting a call to The Zoo could mean absolutely anything, so we had to be prepared for just every eventuality.

We arrived at the house; our wheels screeched to a halt on the pavement out front. I took a momentary gander towards the house before grabbing my equipment and jumping out of the ambulance. What awaited us this time? When we made our way into the property, we found five to ten middle-aged men, drunk off their ass. *Fantastic*, I thought as I scanned the area for threats and began my usual assessment. Then I noticed that one of the individuals was David R., a *frequent flyer,* notorious for calling 911 from a pay phone, laying on the ground, and playing unconscious. Then, when we would get him to the hospital, he'd simply jump out of the ambulance and run away. It was quite an ingenious way of hitching a ride across town to the next bar, but it was one that had wasted our medical resources far too many times. I had nothing against David personally. I understood that his life must have taken a wrong turn, no one grows up planning to stare down the barrel of a bottle every day. But my empathy was outweighed by the fact that his behavior endangered the entire county. An ambulance that was busy chauffeuring him across town for a drink was unavailable for someone who may need it to survive.

With these thoughts zooming around in the back of my mind, I brought my focus quickly back to the incident at hand. David directed us to his friend who had had far too much to drink and demanded we take him to the hospital. I couldn't believe it. *First off, no one tells me who to take to the hospital*, I thought through a veil of deep frustration. *Second, there is no medical reason for this guy to go there.*

While his comrades weren't convinced of his lack of need, I certainly was. The inebriated gentleman was able to answer my evaluation questions, so I felt no obligation to take his drunk ass to the hospital. I even thought of using those exact words to announce my refusal, but decided to hold my tongue for the sake of honor and not wanting to be lectured by my partner about proper etiquette.

Tired of the situation and utterly convinced we weren't needed, Ronnie and I collected our things and made our way towards the door. But before we could reach the exit, David began his usual nonsense. There was no way he would let us leave

The First Line of Defense

without taking his friend. I put the med bag between David and myself and pushed my way past him. Ronnie followed, seemingly just as eager to remove himself from the situation. After all, we can't just go Chuck Norris on whomever we like, we're EMTs.

We finally managed to escape into the front yard. We threw our bags in the ambulance, jumped in, and locked the doors. This was necessary because David had the reflexes of a lion pouncing his prey on the African plains, and he had consumed more alcohol than I could stomach in a week. In another life he could have been an athlete, but now he was just a dude bent on vengeance against the evil EMTs who refused to play taxi driver for his buddy.

Before we knew it, he was hanging off the side of the ambulance trying to punch the windows in to get to us inside. We were trapped like sardines in a fishing net. Many thoughts raced through my mind, like how a judge would look at the situation if I had jumped out and handled the invader myself. But there was something else that captured my attention, something that an EMT waits his whole career for, and it was this fateful night that we got to push *the orange button*.

The orange button is a legendary device reserved for life-and-death situations. It gives the person who pushes it ten uninterrupted seconds to broadcast over the whole county, blocking out every other radio transmission. It's a distress beacon, a cry for help, designed to let the police know we needed them. The situation had gotten so far out of hand it was time to take action. I slammed the orange button and held my breath.

In that brief moment of silence a million thoughts flew past my mind's eye. It's strange, but wherever we are there is always noise, whether cars, people, or the night critters frolicking about the vast wilderness, nothing is completely still. But in that moment, when I pushed that orange button, the whole world seemed to fall silent.

My pondering was short-lived however, as the radio transmissions cut out and we had open air to call for help. "Ambulance 1 to Cumberland Med, Can you start a 16 unit this way? We have an individual attempting to break the windows in the ambulance. I repeat, send PD!" What happened next was both astonishing and painstakingly hilarious. Just seconds after our radio transmission was broadcast across the county for all to hear, we heard police sirens coming around the corner of the entrance to The Zoo. As if by a force of magic, they heard our cry and like a knight in shining armor they arrived. I was left speechless by the response. I knew they would arrive soon, but I had never imagined they would be able to get here so fast. There must have been a squad car literally around the corner when we put in our call.

Nevertheless, David was not to be dissuaded from the war he was raging on the exterior of our ambulance. He was like a hungry Pitbull who had been separated from an eight-ounce rump steak after weeks of being deprived of food. He knew what he wanted and was willing to do anything to get it and nothing, not even the police, was going to stop him.

One officer dove heroically into action and grabbed David by the scruff of his jacket. With all of his might he pulled him off the ambulance and they both landed on the ground with a thud. A wrestling match that would leave WWE fans gasping ensued as the officer used complicated techniques to try and restrain David. Watching through the window I was amazed at the skill David brought to the table. He once again seemed like an athlete, able to use his quick reflexes to overcome his opponent. Intrigued by the spectacle, and feeling like the situation was being handled, Ronnie and I got out of the ambulance. It was one of the best decisions I ever made.

The officer and David had been struggling for a period of time and it seemed neither was getting the upper hand, but this particular policeman wasn't going to be outdone. With a high-pitched shriek he jumped to his feet and, infused with adrenaline, he yelled "DO YOU WANNA RIDE THE LIGHTNING?"

I was perplexed, but his question struck me as incredibly funny and I could feel a ball of laughter making its way up my esophagus. Before I had the chance to release it the officer pulled out his standard issue TASER and took aim. David's expression switched from anger to dread in mere milliseconds as he saw the inevitable consequence of his actions hurl towards him in the form of two prongs carrying a devastating charge. But as he crouched into a ball to somehow dodge the pain he was about to feel, the charged fangs of the TASER simply bopped against him and fell to the ground, like a paintball off a Tyrannosaurus Rex.

David stood there, frozen in fear, doubtless contemplating whether it would not have been better for him to stay indoors and have another cold one, but he eventually realized that the weapon had failed in its mission and that his thick leather jacket, made from apparently impenetrable cowhide, had saved him.

Emboldened by the misfire, David darted straight for his opponent. Now it was the officer's turn to be rescued. His partner, who had been left in the car presumably to call for back-up, dashed to the rescue like a firefighter to a cat in a tree. Together they overpowered the rage-fueled David and grabbed his arms and legs to transport him to their vehicle. But David wasn't done yet. Like a champion boxer in his title-weight match, he had one more bout left in him. Squirming ferociously, he managed to get a leg loose and reared a devastating back kick towards the unlucky officer holding his feet. The target: the officer's family jewels.

Ronnie and I turned around, not wanting to see what was about to happen. After a few more minutes of scuffling we heard the car door slam shut and there was silence. David had been defeated and the officers stood victorious, but for us the moment lasted longer as we stood there staring at one another. Eventually I could no longer hold it in and yelled, "DO YOU WANNA RIDE THE LIGHTNING?"

We couldn't stop laughing. The officer who had coined the phrase revealed a glimpse of embarrassment and then, stirred by the turmoil of our laughter, expressed a hint of comedic appreciation. It was the perfect way to end a very dangerous situation. That one phrase would in our hearts and minds become solidified eternally, being reiterated whenever we were lucky enough to tell our story. But all laughter aside, we were thankful for the help we were given that day. Those officers left us with a deeper appreciation for the police and the service they provide. They had come to our rescue, all we had to do was push the orange button.

Chapter Eleven
BACK FROM DEATH

There are some things in this world that, no matter how hard I try, I cannot begin to understand. An EMT is someone who uses the advances in medicinal science to prevent the deterioration of someone's health. It's a process that can be tracked, measured, taught and duplicated. Having such a basis for the work I do every day is grounding. It allows me to trust in the process as I knew it would work. But sometimes that place be-tween what is and what is not can become blurred.

It was a normal Tuesday. I had been assigned my reg-ular six-to-two daytime shift and was partnered with Sharen, one of my favorite work colleagues. She was an amazing EMT, a twelve-year veteran at the service, and one of those providers who had seen practically everything there was to see. I typically looked forward to our shifts together because they were always eventful. Even if we didn't turn a wheel, we still had fun. Just like every Tuesday, we had prepared our gear and were doing the rounds in the ambulance. Sharen and I had de-vised ways to keep ourselves entertained between calls. Though it may seem like a life of constant action and adventure, the truth is that emergency medical technicians you do a lot of waiting. We had placed a plastic cup from one of our favorite lunch spots on the center console and were throwing crumpled napkins into it for points. Just as I was about to rack up my third win in a row, we were given the instruction to confirm a person's death, known as a class-2 expiration. And with that, the day took a grueling turn. "Ambulance 2-1 responding" I answered to the dispatch center, assuring them that we would handle the situation. We strapped in and hit the pedal.

I had traveled this route many times and knew exactly what to expect from the roads. Luckily, at this point in the day it was smooth sailing as most of the commuters were already in their offices. It took less than five minutes to arrive. Sharen and I shared a grim look. Even though seeing a lifeless body was something that happened rather frequently, it's never easy. We mustered our resolve, jumped out of our trusted ambulance, and strode towards the house. As we approached the front door I felt a slight chill in the air. It was a fresh morning, nothing out of the ordinary, but I remember feeling as though things were a little cooler than they had been back at the station.

We were greeted by a short, somber woman who appeared to be placed in the front yard almost as a decorative piece, like a garden gnome. Her hair was gray and curly and her kitchen apron hung far below her knees. She introduced herself as the deceased's neighbor, the one who had alerted us to the unfortunate incident. "We typically see Ruth every morning when she comes out to get her mail. As you can see, she hasn't gotten her mail in two days. She gave us a key to her house. This morning

I went in to check on her and I found her laying on the bathroom floor. There's no way she can be alive, so we called you guys."

The distress in her voice was clear. It isn't easy seeing someone dead; it's even harder when it's your friend. "Did you guys touch anything?" I asked as I noticed what appeared to be her husband at the side of the yard.

"No, we left everything exactly how we found it and came back outside," she chirped, as though she was winning a prize for crime-scene management. It was strange the way she had held herself up until that point, and I felt as though something strange was going on.

I put my suspicions away because, analytically, this case sounded pretty open-and-shut. Sharen and I made our way into the old wooden residence. As we got inside we were greeted by an odor that I could only describe as moth balls and vegetable soup. It was a delicate concoction of aromas that perfectly captured the style of the home. Old chandeliers drooped from the ceiling like overgrown stalactites, and the oaken bannisters leading towards the second floor looked as though they had been pulled from an old Viking ship. The entire residence gave me a strange feeling. It could have easily been used as a Victorian-era movie set.

Once we had made our way upstairs, we turned the corner into the main bathroom. There, perfectly still on the floor, was the owner of the home, just as the neighbor had said. It appeared that the patient had some kind of a GI issue and bled to death. But it wasn't just that. It looked as though she had crawled toward the phone to call 911 but never made it. I had never seen so much blood, from floor to ceiling. It looked like a scene from CSI.

I knelt down next to her and checked her pulse. As I suspected, there wasn't one, and she was cool to the touch. She had probably been dead for a while. I asked Sharen to confirm what I had established while I began writing my notes for the coroner. As I wondered if the poor lady had any family I felt a strange sensation on my lower leg. I thought Sharen had brushed against me while I was taking my notes. When I looked up I made eye contact with Sharen—on the other side of the room. A shudder shot up my spine and I screamed "OH MY GOD" like a twelve-year-old girl. The patient that two trained medical professionals had pronounced dead had grabbed my right pant leg. Sharen knelt down next to her and almost rolled backwards through the patient's dried blood. I grabbed for my mic to call for assistance, but my hands were shaking so bad I couldn't keep my fingers still enough to press the right buttons. Somehow my rattling limbs calmed just long enough to contact a medic unit for assistance. I ran outside to grab my first-aid bag and a back board. Bill, my boss, pulled on scene with reinforcements. In the blink of an eye we had gone from a run-of-the-mill deceased patient to someone holding on for dear life. With the combined effort of all involved we were able to package the patient and get her to the hospital where she made a full recovery. To this day, I am so glad that this woman managed to overcome death, but I can tell you that terrifying-looking house and a dead woman grabbing my leg will be the stuff my nightmares are made of for the rest of my life.

Chapter Twelve
GUARDIAN ANGEL

It was early December and the frost had begun to settle across the county. Children plodded along in thick coats and oversized scarfs and the grownups didn't want to leave their heated homes for more than a minute. It was unusually cold and the forecast told us to expect a snow storm. I love the snow; it reminds me of building forts and hurling snowballs with the neighborhood kids. But today the cold white blanket that draped the Midstate would bring something far less nostalgic and joyful.

It was around two-thirty in the afternoon and school was out for most of the kids. They flocked all across town desperate to get home to central heating and a warm meal. But just as the bulk of them were on the move the whiteout reared its head. Heavy snow fell like a tsunami. Visibility was reduced to ten yards or less.

My partner and I had been on the job for quite a while when we received the call: A young boy, ten years old and may a hundred and fifteen pounds fully dresses, was crossing the street on the way home from school. The whiteout had caused intense chaos all across town, vehicles were sliding every which way. A white van had gotten out of control and struck the child.

The First Line of Defense

My throat swelled and my stomach knotted. He was hit so hard that he literally got knocked out of his shoes and was thrown twelve feet across the pavement.

We arrived at the scene expecting a huge mess. The vehicle had a large dent on the driver's side and the mirror had been knocked clean off by the boy's head. We had to be prepared for the worst. We did our initial assessment and packaged the patient as quickly as we could. *Hershey Medical Center is only a short drive away*, I thought, hoping that the boy would hang on until we got there. However, my concern soon became astonishment.

While en route to HMC, I once again assessed the patient for broken bones, bleeding, cuts, or bruises. The knots in my stomach had become a dry itch on my hands as I tried to make sense of what I perceived in front of me. This timid child, who could fit into a banana box, who was struck by a three thousand-pound van, was completely injury-free from head to toe. My surprise wasn't overlooked by my medic. He performed his ALS procedure and advised HMC of the patients' condition prior to our arrival, but just like me he could make out no greater signs of injury. We were baffled.

Once we arrived at the hospital, we transferred the patient to the awaiting trauma staff. When we handed him off, a strange feeling overtook me. What had I just witnessed? My partner shook me out of my daze and we returned to the station. Later, when I called to check on the patient's condition, the staff expressed the same astonishment. He was completely fine, not a hair out of place, not a bruise or a broken bone. I can't explain it. I can't fathom how this boy, who left visible damage to a large vehicle, had nothing wrong with him. I was shell-shocked.

It doesn't happen often, but almost every EMT I have met has a story like this, unexplained miracles that litter the medical landscape. It's difficult to understand how it could happen, and maybe it's just paranoia and a lot of unexplained natural phenomena, but at the very least it creates an appreciation for something greater in your heart and mind to witness something that should be impossible happening to benefit another person. It makes you believe in guardian angels.

Chapter Thirteen
DOMESTIC

Some of the most tragic things that I see in my line of work are domestic fights. They represent everything that can go wrong in a relationship and often lead to dire consequences. In my experience, I've found that same-sex domestic fights are more common than domestic fights between men and women. I don't know if this is backed up scientifically, but it seemed to be the norm in my county.

There was a lesbian couple that, unfortunately, we visited every week and every visit was the same. They would fight, and one of them would make a half-assed suicide attempt, the kind that's done strictly for the sake of getting attention. She was a diabetic and her go-to method was taking all of her insulin, knowing we would get there to fix the problem with an amp of D50 (Sugar). It was extremely sad to see people go to such lengths for the sake of attention from another person. Co-dependence to this degree can be extremely dangerous and toxic to any relationship.

It was a Thursday afternoon when we got the call to visit our regulars. There had been a massive fight and one of the two women was in imminent danger. When we arrived, we found the

The First Line of Defense

woman talking to herself in her beaten-down old car. We approached the vehicle to see what was going on and to attempt to contact the patient, but she ignored our knocks and calls through the window as if she were in her own little dimension. Luckily, we weren't the only professionals on the scene. Several police officers had been put on stand-by in case of a possible escalation.

After several attempts to open the door had failed we decided to smash the window. The glass shattered into a thousand pieces and the woman gave a shrill shriek that could have raised the dead. We had been advised to stand a little out of the danger zone while the police entered the vehicle but, like a wildcat, we were ready to spring into action at any moment.

After the police confirmed that she didn't have any weapons they gave us the signal. We rushed to her aid and, once again, we were able to bring her back with the help of good old D50.

As the woman's condition began to fully stabilize, and the biggest worry drifted behind us, her partner appeared at the doorway. Throughout this ordeal she had been holed up in her house unwilling to come and see what the fuss was about. To be honest, I couldn't really blame her. The situation seemed as though it had become more than stressful, bordering on the insane. Unfortunately, none of us specialized in relationship counselling and so, after we had finished our work, we left the couple to their own devices.

Domestic

Several weeks later is occurred to me that we hadn't heard from the couple recently, so I assumed they had worked out their problems or they had separated. Charlie and I were finishing up a twenty-four-hour shift on a Monday morning. I'll never forget it because I was exhausted and half-asleep on the passenger side, eyes half shut, drooling slightly, while Charlie drove. Twenty-four-hour shifts can be tough! I was looking forward to my comfortable bed and some well-deserved downtime when I just happened to look up and see a car cross the double yellow and head straight towards us.

In that moment time stood still. As the vehicle approached I dug through my memories as though searching for something specific. Maybe this is what people mean when they say your life flashes before your eyes at the moment of death. It was as if I wanted to see if I had been happy and satisfied with the life I had lived, to be certain that, if I were to perish now, I would leave the world a slightly better place than when I entered it.

Charlie yelled "Holy shit" and jerked the ambulance to the right, sending us just far enough off course that the noses of the cars missed each other by inches. The oncoming vehicle still sideswiped us, but the worst had been averted. In that moment of relief, I almost chuckled as I saw the other car keep driving. How great it must be to be so indifferent and oblivious to almost causing death and destruction, all the while acting as though nothing had happened.

In my frustration I grabbed the mic and called county. "Cumberland med from ambulance 2-1 priority." The term *priority* is reserved for situations in which everyone else needs to shut up so we could talk to county. It also means that everyone with a radio stops what they're doing and listens.

"Ambulance 2-1 go ahead."

"Cumberland from ambulance 2-1 we were just involved in a motor vehicle accident, all occupants are fine however the driver fled the scene. We are just past the Center Street bridge in front of Highmark."

"Stand by 2-1 we are dispatching fire and police." Sixty seconds later a police sped past us, lights and sirens blazing, in a vigorous attempt to find the driver. We later found out that Officer Mathis, someone who we'd had the pleasure of working alongside many times, was just down the street when the call came, so he was quick to respond.

My partner and I were both stunned. An experience like that doesn't just float away into the ether. We sat there trying to catch our breath and analyze what had just happened. "Who do you think that psycho was?" I asked, disregarding any type of professional etiquette.

"No idea, but I'm hoping the cops get a hold of them soon." My partner's answer seemed distant and cold, as though he had transported his consciousness to another plane of existence in order to cope with the situation.

The police tracked down the culprit just a short time later. It was a woman in her late thirties, so inebriated she didn't know her left from right. I was stunned when I found out her true identity: the other half of the lesbian couple. It seemed that she had tremendous issues spanning far more than just her broken relationship.

Years later I found out they had indeed separated, but it didn't end as well as it had begun. One of them couldn't handle being away from the other so she followed her home one day, forced herself into the house, and shot her former lover. Then she turned the gun on herself. It was a tragic end to a troubled relationship.

That couple always stays with me because of their many years of domestic problems. If you look at the pattern you could see it slowly escalate, but no one knew enough to say anything or ask if they could help. We all just assumed it was the typical domestic situation, where one gets beat on but never tries to make a change, and we did the worst thing possible: We wrote it off.

Many things cause you to grow as a person in this job, but none as much as the lives that are lost under your watch. Even though this couple had only been in our care because of fake suicide attempts, it indicated something far deeper. It hinted at the fact that this relationship caused so much suffering that it destroyed their lives. If I had the opportunity to go back and intervene, I would. But we cannot do anything in hindsight. All we

The First Line of Defense

can do is grow and keep moving forward, hopefully helping the next couple from meeting an awful fate.

Chapter Fourteen
CHRISTMAS STEAK

When you're an EMT, working on the holidays is just something you come to accept. At the time of this story I didn't have a wife or kids so working on Christmas Eve wasn't a problem, especially if it meant that someone else could take the evening off. It was a chilly afternoon and my breath turn to fog every time I exhaled. I remember thinking that I should get a pair of gloves for Christmas. It was a sad but also comedic thought: I hated gloves.

My partner and I were sitting in our vehicle attempting to pass the time. My partner, Tim Crouse, was a lot like myself, single with no kids. Unlike me, he was living at a local fire Crouse because he had just moved to the area.

Tim and I started our shift at two p.m. and, so far, it had been rather uneventful. I'd come to expect this from working other holidays. They're slow for the most part, but you do get the occasional breathing problem or sick person. "Should we get some Christmas dinner later?" my tall scruffy partner said as he looked into the distance, scanning the horizon for something potentially interesting.

The First Line of Defense

"Sure, but I want to eat something of substance, something filling" I said as I was reminded of my growling stomach. I wasn't in the habit of eating breakfast and I had once again forgone the most important meal of the day.

"I know this great steakhouse not too far from here, it's called Hoss's, and they make some of the best steak you've ever tasted," Tim assured me. And so, it was decided that we would go to Hoss's and treat ourselves to Christmas steaks.

We sat down, ordered, and made our way to the salad bar (yes, we also eat vegetables). Both of us had just gotten a couple of bites into our salad when the radio crackled. "East Pennfield Township, 38 Juniper road, class 3 for a sick person."

"Ambulance 1-1 responding," I said without enthusiasm. I loved people but sometimes the job was just plain difficult and in that moment I wished that someone else could have responded to the call.

As I swallowed the little salad I'd been chewing, I waved down a waitress and explained that we had to leave. She looked at us like we were superheroes, dashing off to save someone's life. I can't say that it didn't feel invigorating to have somebody look at me like that. No one needed to know that, in actuality, we were going to pick up someone who hadn't pooped in two days.

The waitress smiled and said, "I'll keep your food warm until you come back." I looked at my partner as if to affirm my internal notions of heroism and we dashed out to help the poor soul. Our tires screeched and we arrived at the residence. Ready to take on the challenge we knocked at the door and were greeted by a little old lady. After some rather odd conversation we packed her up and delivered her to someone more qualified to deal with intestinal excretion. I have to say it was probably one of my least appetizing calls and, all in all, I think saving someone from not pooping is not what one could call glamourous. However, it wasn't going to deter Tim and I from enjoying whatever cold version of our Christmas dinner still waited for us at Hoss's.

After about an hour we returned to the restaurant expecting to find our once-edible food that had been left to fester under heat lamps. Nonetheless, it was food and we were starving. We arrived back in the dining room and searched for the seats we had previously occupied. I don't know why, but it was comforting to return to the table I had previously occupied. Maybe I was just hoping to be recognized as the hero who had gone off to save someone's life. Entrenched in my thoughts, I looked up to see the same smiling waitress.

I snapped out of my reverie and realized that the restaurant was all but empty. I honestly felt bad about coming back on Christmas Eve because I was sure that the young waitress probably had someplace to be other than serving two EMS workers. She grinned and said, "The manager ordered you both new steaks. They'll be right out."

I was beyond surprised. Tim and I were so hungry we would have been perfectly content eating warm shoe leather.

The First Line of Defense

When the time came for the check the waitress said, "The man who was seated behind you before you left paid your bill. He said Merry Christmas and thank you for working when everyone else is with their families."

I couldn't believe it. Twice in such a short amount of time I had been left speechless by acts of genuine kindness. I could tell that Tim felt the same way. I left the restaurant with a new appreciation for the uniform I wore, and the people who see me wearing it. I wasn't just taking some lady who couldn't poop to the hospital, I was helping those who couldn't help themselves.

Chapter Fifteen
THE END

Unfortunately, all good things come to an end. Just like the blooming flowers that bloom in spring for just a few short weeks, so my career as an EMT had to make way for the next chapter of my life. Endings are often sad, but in my case it was something more.

I was nearing the end of an excruciating twenty-four-hour shift. At around three a.m. we were dispatched for a cardiac arrest at the ever popular and often visited old folks' home. We were often sent there for obvious reasons, and it was one of my least favorite places to go.

Traffic was exceptionally light and we arrived at the care home in record time, even before our medic. We hurried along the gravel path that led toward the front door. It seemed like the kind of place that people paid money to be sent to, but for some reason it always gave off an uneasy aura, like something was wrong with the place. We entered the building and stepped on the polished marble floor of the reception room. I always marveled at the interior design; large Greek pillars lined the room, towering over my head. However, I had no time to study the architecture today. Someone's life was on the line.

We made our way down the curved hallway and were met by the nurse in charge. She told us she had checked on the patient around one a.m. and when she checked him again around three she found him in cardiac arrest. She seemed in distress and I was unsure whether she really cared for this patient or if she somehow felt as though she had let herself down. I empathized, but this wasn't the time to mourn our own shortcomings.

I put on my gloves and swiftly entered the patient's room. What I saw when I arrived at his bedside shook me to the core. I froze, trying to make sense of what I saw. I had seen many bodies, but this one was like a punch in the gut. I felt a tap on my shoulder and heard my partner's voice. "Are you alright?" I nodded, but I wasn't okay. There on the bed in front of me was my close personal friend, and my only cardiac arrest save since I started my career.

You might remember him from the first story in this book, the man who had only a single leg and had dropped dead without ever realizing that his heart had stopped. To me, he had become far more than a cardiac arrest save. I had become quite close with him and his entire family because of what he and I had been through together. Over the years they had invited me to birthday parties and anniversaries, I felt like I was one of them. And despite us not living together, or even being related, I felt as though I had lost a member of my own family.

After my initial shock had passed, I resumed with my normal inspections. Sadly, it seemed as though he had been gone

The End

for quite a while. There was no point in starting CPR and transporting him to a hospital when I knew exactly what would happen once we got there. Due to obvious signs of death I decided not to attempt resuscitation. It was one of the most difficult decisions I have ever had to make.

A few moments later the nurse popped her head in to let me know that she had contacted his wife and she would arrive shortly. I had a sinking feeling, but I knew in my heart what I had to do. There was a reason I was in that place on that evening, and I believe it was to show deep support to my friend's wife. We took our equipment back to the ambulance and I told my partner to wait for me. I wanted to be there personally when his wife arrived, and I felt the need to do so alone.

As I stood there, thoughts like *Life can be quite short, can't it? You never know when it will end*, or *How would my family feel if they were to find me dead in my bed?* raced across my mind. Mortality is a difficult pill to swallow. Everybody dies, but that evening I felt as though I had come face to face with death one too many times.

Headlights appeared as my friend's wife pulled into the driveway. She saw me waiting. "He's gone, isn't he?"

I nodded and said yes, explaining how I had found him as I held back the well of emotion. She asked if she could see him. It was a privilege to walk her to her husband's room so she could say a proper goodbye. I left her alone and pulled the

The First Line of Defense

curtain. A moment like that doesn't need to be witnessed by anyone other than husband and wife.

I knew on the ride back that I could no longer continue what I was doing. It wasn't that my time as an EMT hadn't been fantastic and rewarding, it certainly had been. But I felt as though it was time for something new. It was almost like my friend leaving this world was a wakeup call to a different kind of life. That night I had decided, cruising along the same streets I had traveled for years, next to a partner I had sat across from many times, that it was time to gracefully bow out of being a full-time emergency medical technician.

EPILOGUE

And so, we arrive at the journey's end. Being an EMT was one of the most difficult, exhausting, exhilarating, challenging, and joy-inducing experiences one could hope for. It is more than just a cash-job, not that I'm trying to pounce on people who work for the sake of money. It was more like a duty. A duty to care, to serve, to protect lives, and to enrich my community.

I learned a lot from my time in EMS that I don't think I could have learned any other way. No matter where I go and what I do, I will on some level always see people as patients. That may sound odd, but hear me out. Everyone on the planet will go through difficult times. Everyone is going to need help. Almost everyone will get sick or ill. In those moments of stress, of desperate need, what we most desire is someone who is willing to take care of us. Someone who will do everything in their power to help us get better. So I will always be looking to my fellow man as someone to help. And you could be that person. If you're thinking of a career as an EMT it might just be the best decision you ever make.

The First Line of Defense

Saving someone's life is like falling in love. The best drug in the world. For days, sometimes weeks afterwards you walk the streets, making infinite whatever you see. Once, for a few weeks, I couldn't feel the earth—everything I touched became lighter. Horns played at my shoes. Flowers fell from my pockets. You wonder if you've become immortal, as if you've saved your own life as well. God himself has passed through you. Why deny it, that for a moment there . . . God was you.

Bringing Out the Dead

ABOUT TATE YOHE

Tate Yohe has lived many different lives, from chef to EMT to barber, always with the common thread of helping others.

Born in Bradford, a small town in northwestern Pennsylvania, Tate was anxious to explore and experience life. He currently lives in Enola, Pennsylvania with his wife. He enjoys music, playing with his rescued greyhound, and bourbon tasting. His current passion is his documentary series *Chairapy Session* which explores the lives of local heroes sharing their life-altering stories from his barber chair.

CHAIRAPY

When I started barbering I wanted to do something to commemorate my fourteen years of working in emergency services, so I hung my patch and badge on the wall behind my barber chair and the Patch Wall was created. Former coworkers began coming in for haircuts and adding their patches to the wall, then my military clients began to add their military patches and deployment patches. I soon realized that every individual who added a patch to the wall had an amazing story to share, stories from work, deployments, good times, and loss. With *Chairapy* we want to bring you inside the barbershop to share their stories and give you a glimpse of their lives.

Experience *Chairapy!* Scan this QR code or visit
https://bit.ly/3fXKWzx